Time Between Tides

Also by Seán Street

Poetry
Earth and Sky
Figure in a Landscape
Carvings
A Walk in Winter
This True Making
Radio and Other Poems
Radio Waves: Poems Celebrating the Wireless (ed)

Prose
Hampshire Miscellany
Petersfield
Tales of Old Dorset
The Wreck of the Deutschland
The Bournemouth Symphony Orchestra
(with Raymond Carpenter)
A Remembered Land
The Dymock Poets
Concise History of British Radio 1922-2002
Historical Dictionary of British Radio
Crossing the Ether: Pre-War Public Service Radio and Commerical
Competition in the UK

Plays
A Shepherd's Life
Wessex Days
Honest John
Beyond Paradise
Mathias
Day Trip to the Trianon

Radio Drama
The Drift of Time
Procession to the Private Sector
(after David Gascoyne)

Musical Works
(with Douglas Coombes)
The Winter Bird
The Benjamin Dream
Papa Panov's Christmas
The Treasure Trail
The Pied Piper of Hamelin
(with Ward Gardner)
Starbirth
(with Donald Dumbell)
Apostle

Seán Street

Time Between Tides
New and Selected Poems
1981–2009

Rockingham Press

Published in 2009 by
The Rockingham Press
11 Musley Lane,
Ware, Herts SG12 7EN
www.rockinghampress.com

British Library Cataloguing-in-Publication Data

A catalogue record for this book
is available from the British Library

ISBN 978-1-904851-33-2

Printed in Great Britain by the
MPG Books Group, Bodmin and King's Lynn

For Jo, Jemma and Zoë

Acknowledgements

Of the new poems in this collection, the *Evidence* Sequence was originally published as a catalogue which also included complementary work by Paul Hyland, accompanying the exhibition of paintings and prints by Jemma Street and Brian Graham, "Evidence – What Lives Leave Behind", by the Atrium Gallery, Bournemouth in 2003 "The Broadcast" sequence was published in *Scintilla* volume 10, (2006) and subsequently broadcast on CBC Radio 1, Canada in February 2007. Other poems were published in *Upstairs at Duroc, South, In the Criminal's Cabinet, Babylon Burning* and *The Friend's Quarterly.*

The poems selected from work published between 1981 and 1999 are grouped in chronological order according to publication, *Figure in a Landscape* (Outposts Publications, 1981), *Carvings* (Guthlaxton Wordsmith, 1982), *A Walk In Winter* (Enitharmon Press, 1989), and *This True Making* (KQBX Press, 1992). "Shipping Forecast, Donegal" formed part of *Radio – Ten Poems About Sound*, commissioned by BBC Radio 4 and broadcast on that network in 1998. The sequence was published by Rockingham Press in 1999. Also included here from that collection are "Blue Candles", "Above Newton Farm" (first published in *Scintilla 1*), "K595", "God and The Green Man", "Corpus Christi, Oxford", "Charles Darwin at Down House, 1880", "Building a Church 1094" (commissioned to mark the 900th anniversary of the building of Christchurch Priory in 1994, and first published in *South* in October of that year) ,"Still Life", "Three Yangtze Prints" and "Muire na nGael". I am grateful to the publishers of these collections for permission to reprint the poems selected from those books in this volume.

Contents

Poems 2000 – 2009

The Broadcast – A Newfoundland Sequence

Mist Later

Selected Poems 1981 – 1999

NEW POEMS
(2000–2009)

The Dying Weather Girl

Rain again. In February the weather
becomes a state of mind. The savoury
part of the year; broken gardens blow about,
it's hard to hold to a purpose just now.

Cyclonic – the lines come in closer.
I remember my greatest forecasts, weather
as news breaking storm warnings and the charts
burst colour of exclamatory symbols.

Brute images beyond the map earnest
in my eyes, see rain and the sea collide
and I stroke, caress chromakey green, conjuring,
conducting elements to camera,

meteorological mime, my making.
Structural damage is inevitable,
the cold front floods through, the burst water rising
shorting out time until all screens blacken, still.

Isobars compress round the bed, weather
rises, tapping, tapping in from the west
hard against glass, I stumble as the glass falls,
falling, broken gardens fly off and away

into February, black and unseen tides.
Tonight there is heavy rain again, storm force,
there is a deceptive wind-chill factor.
Cold. Clouds deepen, make it grow night too early.

Cliff Fall

Samphire Hoe, Kent
King Lear, Act IV, Scene VI

Gloucester's imagined cliff,
Samphire, murmuring surge,
a dizzy horizon
gleaming along its edge,

sunlight dazzle blinding
a gaze on the far sea,
persuading memory
that it saw a man fall,

time between tides rushing
towards darkness, the first
beginnings of distance
from this chalk's white flower.

He is falling, falling
down into the story
of the rest of his life,
gone into the seascape,

the wide pewter bowl, cold,
dull at the rim, turning,
a single figure framed
in the cliff's spun moment,

seeing the universe
flailing through air bright
for the love of Samphire,
living to tell the tale

that recollection breeds
illusion. Though we may
contest against gulls' flight,
our own self will crush us.

Beneath imagined cliffs
the fact of rock, sullen
under resignation –
inevitable impact –

the final gasp seeing
what we were spinning off
into debris, fictions
broken by gravity.

Late Night

An old man, skin
creased with homeless grime
on the beach near Traitors' Gate
half-lit by Embankment lamps,

drunk staggered a turn
from the water's edge,
fell on the grey shingle,
stared up at us, tried

to swear but could not,
rose to his feet slowly
as if summoning
a last rhetoric –

a rhetoric all but lost –
instead murmured
to himself and Thames
"Are they my children?"

Avalon

In 1626, Sir George Calvert, later Lord Baltimore, made an ill-fated attempt to form an English colony at Ferryland, on the southern coast of Newfoundland, naming it, "The Colony of Avalon." The site has been the subject of excavation. In 1901 Guglielmo Marconi received the first transatlantic wireless message on Signal Hill, St. John's.

Silence. Waiting for a signal to come.
Wind beating into the hill,
interrogating the built stones,
seeking to find them wanting,
and beyond it, silence.

Worse than silence,
the obscuring white noise of time,
burying the fragile message
as the storm covers the remnants
of Baltimore's mansion.

So far to come,
so much mitigates against it,
the sepia of ancient sounds fading,
fading to grey, to finally white.

And finally they come
to dig, seek to ease away years –
as if they could –
uncovering the sweet poignant delicacies
of another life, the futile hope of it.
But as they find things,
somehow the silence grows deeper.

Send me a signal.
Let me know you,
bring me your sibilance,
the *s* of your *yes*
to show me you were here.

Out in the bay something is stirring,
the water boils with change.
Send me morse
as they scratch down to your stones,
raising the dead of the place.

Listen... No.
Just the wind beating into the hill,
only silence beyond
the endless *shh* of the sea.

Of Thought

Thomas Percy, sawyer, died the eleventh of December of thought having slaine a man in Rochester which was the cause, being unknowne unto mee untill a day before he died, that he came on this voyage
(John Guy, Cupers Cove, Newfoundland, May 16, 1611)

I did pray the distance might salve my sin,
that a long sea of sickness and scurvy
would serve me penance, that new skies
would make God forget before
it came to a final confession,
that this place might accept me
without suspicion, with gentle judgement.

It was not so. His own soul confronted
a pain so great life could not support it,
and as the first winter came, hardening
the ground's heart, the thought's cancer
took him, five months ashore at Cupers.

Each our own archaeologist,
searching below surfaces we find
crimes buried as the layers build.
We dig for facts mercifully sinking.

They had seen no reason for it
as he wasted but when they buried
him in the new found earth the canker
of conscience soaked the virgin soil,
breaking its cold Eden innocence
with a virus left by memory,
the decomposition of him worming
its secret into the very rock;
the stain of inhaled infection -
Cain's contagion spreading his guilt -
seeping out through unsuspecting land.

Each our own archaeologist, we seek
circumstantial evidence, extenuation
to absolve us. And yet it takes but a germ
faithful over the long interrogation
of voyage, breeding its capacity
to outgrow guilt's sacred disease
of self-encounter, the sanctification
of apology, the possibility of redemption,
to incriminate beyond forgiveness
the exposed fact, blood-raw as red bone,
the thought of the act, admission gasping,
its wide fish eye swimming always at us,
squirming, malignant under all this time.

Quaker Poem

George Dannatt – Ikon of Silence 1, Oil on Canvas, 2001

The door opened into a space.

I heard stillness offer itself
towards the shape of a prayer.

Coming out of light, we return
after all.

In the meantime there's
silence, white paper between words
going where noise of words cannot,
present even under these days,
a space just beyond the next door.

Heatwave
Hartford, Connecticut

While the car was part of a gridlock
they suddenly heard the tyres sink in the road.
Later he noticed the limp leaves,
the stillness, a distant train, no birds.

It was the true absconding of light,
a sky grown huge by emptiness,
darkening as metaphor for silence –
it was the distancing that evening.

He noticed there was something else
happening, a sub-text, all at once
another meaning, previously so
parenthetical as to be an unheard murmur.

Almost too late there was understanding
that the melting tar and the changed sky
were not part of his day, nor him,
but the flavour of a place where he was a stranger.

These things are not there because we see them –
It is all the habit of nature, a routine
in which the Universe cannot help itself.
The moment after the eyes glaze
there will be a warm day or cold,
and the tide will carry things inland
or out down river far, far away,
beyond the one left standing,
imagining he still sees.

Garbo Develops a Photograph
(April, 1990)

Fluctuate image in the red of darkness.
She said "It is my picture now." The flickering
Silver through romantic stone, sex, sea, gothic forests
in fog, smoke, snow, classical memory of a lake,
deserted, lit through moon-struck birches -

these things evaporate. Her picture. She thought
"I am not singular if you catch me literal.
Let suggestion seep over, like blood." And so
preservation into parody. Keeping a distance
beyond a wall becomes art in the basement,

a place where lines centre then fragment.
Evolving in the pungency of darkrooms,
ego has a final say, a grey God steps back,
and behind the shadow is another
truth in the ruby dusk. "My picture."

The tone of a pose across hills, cloud
a reflection. But here at last's control.
She might have said "Comb out self
and find the invisible." Art's face
always rang back at her. Always,

until this chemical sunset. Now, oozing
ectoplasm develops back beyond
childhood, back to the perfect shape,
alone in the red of darkness
without silver message or implication. Blank.

The Sacrifice

i.m. Andrei Tarkovsky

There is no remembrance of former things. Neither shall
there be any remembrance of things that are to come with
those that shall come after.
                              Ecclesiastes

Nato planes have accidentally bombed a hospital.
                         News broadcast, May 1999

I

In spite of ourselves we return to the same place
simply because we cannot recall ourselves
ever to have been there before. If we did
we would not come back again.
It is why things always end in the same way.

II

I blow a speck of dust from my hand.
I watch it drift, tiny – so tiny – up.
It seems to hang for a moment then gently
it falls, slowly, softly through the late night
onto the table. Silent. Infinitely delicate.

At the same instant somewhere brute bombs
blast into bone and blood through stone and tin.
Surgical air-strikes. Surgical. Missiles
like space-ships into children.
Why are they hurting me? Have I not been good?

III

Listen. Nothing. It is only the night
beating in my ears. I had thought for a moment
I heard crying. I thought I heard
something strange above me coming closer.
It is nothing. Only the house around me.
Only my children sleeping.

IV

Bombs into blood and bone. What a way
to celebrate Christ. What a way
to cross a threshold, to mark a millennium,
to close or open a door, to punctuate time.
But then again, why not?

V

Cancer and I are old friends.
He has spoken to me often through the eyes
of the people who made me. An old friend.
He's welcome, but like all guests
there's an etiquette to be observed; to be polite
he should know his time. Mostly he does, he understands.
And given that, he's a gentleman. He leaves time
to organise things. He's civilised.
He's not a bomb.

VI

Thank you god of future times for the gift
of forgetfulness. Why would I want to remember this?

VII

What is a gift if it is not a sacrifice?
If a gift has not entailed a sacrifice
how can it be a gift?
            What is it worth?

Mrs. Bates

(Psycho)

I'm Norman's mother.
A good boy, most of the time.
He carried me gently.

The director on the other hand
I did not like. He made the whole thing
a black joke. It wasn't a joke.

(I loved it when she screamed
there in the basement,
when I turned. Oh yes, I turned.)

What did you think I was?
A prop? Something cooked up
in Design? No. I'm not a joke.

Sometimes dreams come true.
Where did you think I went
after the film was made?

Sometimes dreams come true.
I know. I was young once.
Mine was to star in the movies.

I'm Norman's mother.
One day you'll look like me,
but you'll be dead of course.

I love it when they scream.
Sometimes dreams come true.
Mine will be the last face you'll see

tonight, after the light.
Just before sleep, as you turn,
you'll see me. And scream.

Projector

(Persona, Ingmar Bergman*)*

It's a voice from the blood round the brain's stem
keeps things focused for the point-of-view shot
of the wine I'm drinking now – taste, colour.

Meanwhile, outside this warm diegesis
there's another camera framing me,
a retrospective for the congealing.

A second after death the flickering
footage will record my cooling, staring,
film in my projector chattering loose.

Diegetic and non-diegetic;
I listen to the blood, drink smooth red wine,
tasting the colour the brain's stem sends me.

Pipa

That sound – and you are here again
beside me. Ancient music evokes you,
your ghost haunts walls, our days together
gone – only the echo now, white snow in spring.

A world away, beyond reach,
I imagine you somewhere, your smile
for someone else as the music chimes on
over cold grey England. Distance is Time,

Time, a long road growing
longer without me even moving.
A lengthening road between us, snow
melting, an old song – your spring echo.

Number Stations

1

It was December near Riga,
everything the colour of mist, no voices
as trains dovetailed at still platforms
and the silent crowds from carriages
evaporated across the fields.

Gradually we were decanted
through changes into a soup of suburbia,
simplifying into fields,
the punctuation of ditches enhancing
the strict grammar of Place, undermined
by subversive fog.

That night the clouds made sounds .

2

We have come deep into a forest,
or is it perhaps a desert,
spun through shorting space
to a place where the chants
ring alone, meaning, time
reduced to this,
a memory preserved of how
the crumbled voice box
once sang.

3

A silent track, a spire, transmitting.
I am moving through England in April dusk,
trees edging out of monochrome, day into grey,
passing light, into twilight.

Daventry calling...

Dusk, but the green light of young leaves glows
over seeded fields east towards the broadcast of night.

Not quite here yet though.
England in April dusk.
Tranquil before the voices start.

4

I tune in. White noise again.
Nothing but electric sea.
No words, no music.
Just æther's endless ebb
until in the end even the voices
grow still and all tapes end.

5

Darkness. Distant thunder.

The clocks stop.

Listen...

Finally the sound of rain
        whispering on still water.

Within Walls

Charleston

There is a moment when the crowds go,
the guides close the shutters, rooms adjust
their eyes to the dusk, the fish outside
trance and silence seeps under the sill.

A long moment before the murmurings
stir, shadows within shadows move.
The patterned pastels swim down
passageways, voices, voices.

The Bells are at home and the last door
shuts – the house regains itself.
Keynes upstairs, not to be disturbed,
Grant in the studio, Forster on the stair,

somewhere the Stephen sisters
sharing, rehearsing their sorrows,
and soon Grace will signal tea, all in
the shift of awoken memory.

But outside there's a garden ghost
by the bean canes, listening
in vain amongst the apple trees,
near the poppies at the flint wall,

imagining the cry of a recalled face
at a window while the colours drain
to a dark place, her desperate arms
outstretched through the upper glass,

the walls' paper blotting
vermilion, lilac, silver, mauve,
pulling the song from flowers,
feeding a silence back.

You cannot forever be
safe within walls, ask the ghost,
ask the ghost in the garden
faithfully listening.

Under Firle you're in this womb,
over the blood of the poppy fields
you know there's another place.
It's just the house talking,

You know what will happen.
Don't listen to the place. Sometime,
somewhere, we all leave our spirits
behind. In the end, we all must go.

War of The Worlds
(*Dissertation*)

October dusk, the wireless glowing,
you with the BBC sunset full of
gentile hymns, while from New Jersey
the Mercury Theatre destroys America
in a CBS commercial hour.

1938, a good year for nightmares,
safely sepia now, drowning
in a Pye set's domestic seascape,
sinking down, down, through
psalms into Artie Shaw, Munich.

The war between that world
and our civilised academe sets
refugees with forged passports a-sail
over waters of walnut to lost even-light,
secretly seduced by warm valves' glow.

We are alone each in our own shadow;
suddenly you are standing at the door
of your father's room, coming too late
but in time to find him the morning after,
his bedside lamp and the transistor still on,

still on after so many years' listening-in,
sound too intimate to be rational;
invaders from Mars make us imagine
voices but they're no substitute
for the real thing, the long witness.

You're right to get the *zeitgeist*,
to gain an authentic sense of the reality
creating a context for all this.
The fact is, it won't happen – radio
is too pictorial, too personal.

The student in you bravely turns
horrors to emotionless theory,
and here am I supervising and so
condoning these fictions, as if we invented
them, exonerating us – absolving.

Gradually we are washed ashore
on this beach of objectivity, confused
by Time's shifting documentary,
subverted by the old enemy
memory, nostalgia, history channels,

only to be cross-examined by
a dead smile, a survivors' time shared,
existing in a theatre of the air, the lampshade
still warm, like skin, parental whispers,
faded radio tides, suns that won't set.

Specifics

There might be a stone
among the rest

in an old wall
the same as the others but
for the fact you noticed it.

That brings commitment.
Beware the discomfort of eye contact
with a specific –

it could be speaking the unspeakable
beyond something as civilised
as a strategy, a euphemism,

somewhere safely abstract ideas
of sophisticated policies
while children burn.

Fen Swimming

(Helpston)

Faced with this chosen expanse
where is the choice, I ask you?
It has to be that I breast
hissing seas in from The Wash,
a Spring flood-moon's love-making
making the body stretch out
to bisect my horizon.

Home's a shore where the Snipe's nests'
squalor aspires to light's arc,
here, from Botolph's beach, skies reach
beyond the mercy of land.
Out past Glinton to Barnack –
for who knows where deeps begin? –
Fosdyke, down Welland and on.

On – beyond gulls' screams fading
and memories of a home
where all oceans ooze, seeping
their symptoms down leyline dykes'
veins – I'll float out with the tide,
exchange flatness of waters,
ebb to new infinity.

Helen Thomas in Epping Forest

A sound pushed like paper under a door
was all that you left of yourself for me,
unmaking the shape of us. While you saw your way,
the leafless window promised me nothing
in its changing tone-songs, Easter
after Easter already written, imagined
through the fogged silence of woodland,
its ally in a conspiracy of short days.

And I've had to live with that prophecy,
body of a solitary alive
in a rain that has once too often slushed
memory seeking a dusk poem
in the prosaic glare of grey light.

All this remains in the knowledge of winds
that still blow now and then over the place
making me a ghost there. In the morning
hereafter there's a dress on a bed
and a naked silhouette in white light
by the window as if it happened yesterday
when the snow's stillness brought us together,
the iambics of you walking away
evoking the last sounds we made of love.

The Broadcast

'The Fisheries Broadcast', known to Newfoundlanders simply as 'The Broadcast', CBC1, St. John's – "possibly the longest-running program in North American radio history".

1. The Broadcast

Suddenly somewhere a radio is talking to itself
as crisis succeeds routine, the wave strikes,
the heart for no reason stops or the moose
steps out unseen on the twilight road.

For the rest, there is this daily prose,
a part of us now, a station of the day,
taking us beyond industry into identity,
edging itself over the years towards a poetry.

5.30 in Newfoundland, 5 o'clock in much of Labrador.
CBC Radio debates with the wireless waves,
with ebbing signals of tides, shorelines breaking,
holds dialogue with the nature of the place.

And during a programme's tide of greet and goodbye
crisis may succeed routine; some radios in
Newfoundland and parts of Labrador may now be
talking to themselves. For those of us left, there's this.

2. Naming

Belle Isle, Come-by-Chance, Cabot Strait.
Every name's a story, but weathers change,
tides overwrite and meanings ebb.
Happy Adventure, Great Paradise, Fortune Head.
Every name's a story until new stories come
where men after men die fighting the sea for a harbour.

Funk Island, Mistaken Point, Snakes Bight,
Savage Cove, Wreck Cove, Deadman's Bay.
Every name's a story.
Every day, new stories come.

3. Squid Jigging
Hickman's Harbour, Random Sound
For Gilbert Penny

The squid come slurping, squirting
their fury into the bed of the boat. Gulls wait,
an eagle hangs, there's a whale six waves away.

Gilbert fishes to the radio. *Some voices.* Pearl sky,
grey sea, but the firs are dragging the night inland.
On the land you know what's there, what you see.

The squid come slurping, frantically
flexing colour, a last camouflage against dying,
and then, dying, they turn to pearl too, their eyes bead.

The whale has gone, silently. *You know what the land*
shows you. Here we don't know what's twenty feet
from us, down there. Gilbert looks back at the bay.

Dusk, and somewhere ashore, the moose
will be on the road, shadows emerging from the firs.
The lights of Hickman's Harbour start to show.

The eagle beats towards home, gulls give up where the whale
was but now is not, perhaps. Gilbert's radio loses its signal.
The squid are still. The boat's bed blackens.

4. Twillingate

Two Young Fishermen were drowned
News Report, CBC Radio 1, October 2000

The bay's curve phases sounds
until they all cry like gulls.
But I swear I heard your voice.
Tie yourself to the boat.

It goes on happening,
tides will happen.
Tie yourself to the boat,
give them at least a body.

Then through the sea wash radio:
Never heed the gulls,
these are dead sounds
phased to make you wonder.

Now we encounter the elements
through regulation, seek to civilise
with rules; technology
pretends sophistication.

But in the end, it's down to a voice –
At the worst, tie yourself to the boat.
A reality. *Give them back a body.*
Tides will happen. Go regulate the sea.

5. Heart's Content Cable Station

The cable is almost silent now. Here's the end and start
of a thousand miles from and to Valencia slipping
into and out of the sea, just the voice of the dead
rising and sinking, moving gradually closer then away
'till the sounds are lost in sepia a mile down.

The beach rusts as the dead cable bleeds,
shredding throats' ebbing song back into static,
and beyond, the deepest silence never heard,
far from the storm and shout of human making,
back into the miles-deep sea, submerging to stasis.

6. L'Anse aux Meadows

There comes a time when Time stops
and walls are no longer relevant,
when in one flash we step
from these tiny cramped days
into vast pearl light spreading
across an enormous room,
no walls visible.

Dimsdale's Box

Gilbert Collection, London

Gold snuffbox, with pink diamonds, presented to Nathaniel
Dimsdale by Catherine the Great or perhaps her son, Grand
Duke Paul, after Nathaniel's father, Thomas, inoculated
them against smallpox, 1768

New light opens the box.
Look, it opens to air the spark
of the rose diamonds.

                  (The livid red
softens, heals, grows beautiful
and the cool flowers shimmer.)

Golden antiquity, enduring as ever,
unfading, bright in the new light,
as bright now as long-lost
thankful eyes, as perfect almost
as a saved life, as borrowed time,
a gift to honour a loan, just a loan.

Today they would see proven
some sort of hope in the continuing glitter,
a metaphor, chance of another miracle,
light that opens the box.

(In the dark, the rose egg hatches dazzle,
grows bright as diamonds spread pocked spark
and flicker, jewel-graffiti, over us,
outliving us, leaving their mark.)

An Old Country

St George's Chapel, Windsor

Too much responsibility, all this
big death, huge dates, history. Where in this,
the so perpendicular gothic flesh
of fan vaulting, escutcheons, oak stalls,
where's promised eternity beyond rank?

But a half-glimpsed flicker, an eye's corner,
the shadow of a memory, or light
on an opening window, something there's
suggested at the foot of tradition
when the stone goes quiet for a second.

A long moment when the prayer churches
say for themselves after the priests have gone –
the secret prayer locked deep in the place –
becomes perhaps heard, perhaps possible,
timeless light flashed for an instant on glass

Timeline

Weather and light outside the window
remind the room of the time and itself.
In here I measure things by invented means.
Mostly it is the ticking of my grandparents' clock –
the hands say afternoon, the afternoon says autumn.
I categorise the track of routine, monuments of events.

The year and I have come to our eight pm –
at one thirty October light turns its own corner.
It's time to take a break, time for a bite,
habit has given this part of the day a purpose,
the rest is the perspective angles of shadows make
and any metaphors I choose to find in it.

For all of us not so far to go as we have come
but still some miles to travel, things to be done.

Mist Later

The patient is showing symptoms of Vascular Dementia

I
Oak on the Corner

Each day on the window's television
it is last and first
night and morning,
this dusk to the next dawn,

seeded before this road,
it aspires past telegraph
wires, now urban, wholly itself,
rustled by pigeons, magpies, crows
in its world, theirs.

Mine is outside it,
but tree as a thing belongs
to a field of sight
I inhabit for a time,

colour, season through
my expectation, aspiration
through pale damp disappointment,

a proxy wonderment
but more wonderful
is that I am here
to see, to stand on
mutual earth.

I close my eyes, turn away.
It remains present,
Oak roots close and
pushing nearer
under tarmac,
cracking roads
as fumes shrink branches,

2
What Village, What Harbour

Ice under flowers meeting frozen air –
        forbidden thoughts,
words not to be spoken of this conjoining.
Maker – all makers, carpenters,
all makers of bulwarks against nature – these doctors –
pit props only, only enough to stave off collapse
for now – flex muscle, all sinew, makers challenged –
whatever your skill world once energised
more than matches you.

Moving across the flood plain a new perfection.
Can it be music?
                It might indeed be music, a cold
music growing colder.
Such austerity is beautiful,
But the music of diagnostic fact contradicts a summer.
        As light fails, each thing becomes
its own world, shadows build emphasis
but each was always alone.
Sliding over the lawn, cold front promises a blue sky,
But moving through accumulations towards an inevitability.

First imperceptible voile across understanding.
Together in your garden, your lost smile –
I turned away because I could not speak.
First fingers of frost as the glass falls.

Twenty one roses on the Standard bush by the kitchen door.
This October's ice is early – roses but no leaves,
cold crawls in. No leaves – all goes to make a final flower.

What is it experiences this?
We have been here before on the shore as a ship

recedes from a place of touching to an infinity.

Pitted against this fade I only ask what bids me think?
The beach wintering, wintered clink of lines on metal masts in the wind.
But I am moving now out over and beyond my own bay,
bucking on chopped water.
The chime of masts fades. Beneath tides' surface
remains a mystery, deep soundless beyond the harbour,
out on the winter sea I forget I quite forget how I set sail,

                                        what I left.

3
The Room

In the dream I am in my house
but it is not mine but one I have seen
many times in other dreams

There is a set of stone steps
the house is grey stone
and somewhere there is sea

and rocks – a headland
There are stairs everywhere
and a wonderful secret room

From memory I long for
the room because it is
what I love the house for

but I cannot find the way
in and in the dream you tell me
no you know we cannot.

4
Conversation

If your life has been a book
then these sounds are what's left
of its pages – against the cream gloss hospital wall
your huddled foetus echoes memories in phrase-lengths,
a line of urgent babble transmitted
by desperate eyes.

The places of life flash past
and are gone. You talk quickly,
quickly and half to yourself
as though to speak slowly or to stop
would be to allow a fatal silence.

If your life has been a book
then here are scattered torn fragments
caught by winds, flung
and flying around the ward's twilight
until finally it grows dark.

Donaghadee

Waves so slight on shore it is like dissolving,
grey it is, stolen from everything around me
in the grammar of my history, the sea
still slithering between fact and remembering.
Grey shingle, a terrace of cottages ringing
and unpeopled, grey light, a grey tree –
greyness is all I recall of Donaghadee,
as far from me now as you from it when, singing
your memory, you warned me don't go back,
and I haven't. But if we were to meet
again now this would be the place alone
to test adjective, verb and noun on the old track
of recollection. Yet there are only my feet
left to walk now, and silence at the centre of stone.

Fog Music
San Francisco General Hospital

Out beyond the blind sand
deep creatures rise unseen
through night shrouds,
mourning warnings
through a caul of mist
over the brush and rush of invisible tides.

The Trauma Center glows silver
reflected back by the curtain,
a monitor hoots a rhythm,
calling sad counterpoint
back to the milk night. Pods of blood
decant through grey plastic veins.

On Pacific Beach the West Coast
stares out across the fault line,
looking for something
where there's nothing to see
before west becomes east.
10.00 pm, and the ward dusks.

Earthquake weather.
Sand footprints glow
phosphorus for a moment.
Unseen, sea becomes smoke.
Perhaps it is to break the silence
that the dark makes radio and sings

fog music the texture
of soft gauze, siren tropes
hiding the slow grind
of stirring tectonic plates.
Some sorrows belong to us,
some we share.

Through widening cracks,
The fog seeps in, bathing
silent struggles, tubes,
deep scarlet draining,
Fading to grey as even
the needle's interrogation blurs.

Waves from recollection.
On and on the Bay's elegy –
discord, harmony, plainchant –
behind the ward machine's
sharp soprano. Sound,
memory, finally just sound,

the same grey inside and out,
awaiting the earth's next tearing.
The continuity's in the unseen,
the waves beyond cello light,
the hoot and moan somewhere out there,
creatures, moon-eyed, chorusing through shrouds.

Mid-morning, it all becomes clear.
One by one the voices,
the low adagios silence. Inside,
the monitor sings on solo.
The routine of mortality,
the brush and rush of invisible tides.

Evening, Canary Wharf

1

Oh we are handsome things
in our dugouts

shouting up at light
then powering down

blustering out
suddenly to be cut

by ice turning
the estuary's bend

the savage channel
persuading *get real*.

2

What's left behind
is frail darkness,

a purpose ended,
but somewhere

preserved amidst neon
in the paved city,

a small light
on the road

catches a girl's glance
bored from the bus –

blue, a curve of red,
a moment's monument.

3

Reflected
in forsaken towers

a man with no home
sitting, singing

quietly to himself
embracing a past,

an expertise once his
an ancient wood saw
his visible spirit

held to himself,
rocking to sleep,

staring back
at mirror glass

in pale radiance.
Inhuman light.

I Stood Outside In The Rain

Timothy Evans, a tenant at 10, Rilington Place, London, was hanged, 9 March, 1950, for the murder of his wife and daughter. He was later posthumously pardoned and John Christie convicted of the crime.

I stood outside in the rain
as night moved on towards
something more literal.
This was when to be human
was to be part of light,
and darkness was a felony
in which I was complicit.

There was a time when a voice
more than the scribbled word
made a truth out of things.
I could not begin to believe
that this would lead me to
any idea outside that of
simply learning how to lie.

But always the sound of rain
drummed on the oblique glass
of the loft light above me,
winters' bleak poetics,
me hiding here, trying
to circumvent the cold fronts,
a part of another's dark.

Evidence
What Lives Leave Behind

1. Graffiti

It is just where the marks appear
that we come closest to transparency.
Out of the air the beat of a pale wing
makes a form on us for a moment,
the light interrupted, complemented
by shadow, its recollection
a revelation, showing matter
to be a window.

2. Staircase
After a set of prints by Jemma Street

Treader
Step over-writes step
forming created shapes,
a dialogue
blackening through
gradual marks
of divided forms
towards a unity
of shared darkness.

Riser
Japanese flocks occupy
but do not consume this space,
high and distant, becoming flight
on a horizon, so light
they are the airborne face
seen in a haiku's eye,
strokes from a brush quick
as an unminded foot's kick.

3. Brothers' Field
On the land behind the British Museum, called Southampton
Fields, it is said that two brothers once fought to the death for
the love of a girl.

Some pain never dies.
Blood printed in the balding earth,
such hate as nothing will grow on,
stone can only hide, cannot end.
Listen for the shout deep under history.
Some pain never dies.

4. Manuscript, Sonata in A min
For Solo Violin

The sound exists before it is played,
a web, black-dense against white,
light shining through tracery,
winter trees frosted, sunlight
across bought paper,
Bach's own ink, now,
just as it dried where the shadow
of the music first fell.

5. Brassai

Anger. Walls of lines
cover stone, concrete.
Sometimes chance gifts pattern,
something between marks –
shapes, faces – shines through.

6. Elegy for Chet Baker
Died Amsterdam, May, 1988

The warm dark red wine flows
out of the mouth, the trumpet
smooth against the face's map,
the cracked voice like broken stone:
My funny valentine, sweet comic valentine...

The trumpet wine rich and smooth,
and the kind light glows warm
on the gold of the horn,
smooth against the cracked stone
of the broken face. *Unphotographable...*

Europe in Springtime, a new window
every day, tomorrow another town,
another gig, another sidewalk.
The trumpet's wine flows red, warm
out of the mouth. *Stay little valentine, stay.*

7. Glass Dancing
St. Mary Abbots Church, Kensington

The windy sun moves past noon, the tree
at the west door swings to its music
and all over the stained window
the Old Testament troupe
dance too. Jacob, Noah,
their glass brought alive,
resurrected and dancing, dancing
through leaves and the sun's Spring gale.

8. Shadow

If the light is bright enough,
if I can partner it,
I may make a print,
a photograph
to last beyond me on stone
like Hiroshima man.

9. Evidence

The lines cut on this cave wall will fence
my time, give chance a shape, bad or good
like carving under moss in tree wood,
a blurring patina. Evidence,

things I fashion to guard against dark
while guiding those digging for me.
As witness to this naming, you see
my encounter with the same stone, bark.

Reading him, I prove that I'm here now.
Like his handprint, footprint, my spoor
as clue, a light in an open door
forms the best I can show of my *how*.

Down a permanent present gutter
new dynamics will always happen.
That said, all blame and praise in this thin
place should hear past voices' prayer utter

echoes up through to our stammered day.
Inexact images define us
but continuity's kinship, trust
across time. Reshaped, this DNA.

Touchdown on an Unknown Planet

We were talking
during our final descent, backing down
into our own fire, watching,

pinpointing receding stars,
crossing an empty night
over so much silence.

Beyond the window
dust and stone and famine
loosed up at the cold sky
debated our right, our purpose

in being here. We had interrogated
that very thought, stems
from a broken plant.

All this way
for another desert.

The Tower
(Harlech)

Dictation of light,
shadows, bright air.

In the morning
first light touches stone
and the shadows
begin yet again.

In the morning
a whispered ebb
drowned by arrogant
white glare.

Dictation of light,
shadows, bright air,
the calm water-light,
the dark's contradiction.

In the morning
something flickers, the air
off the water
glances brightness across dusk.

Delicate feather and cut,
the transparency floored
by the rusting jagged edge,
the arc of flight trampled.

At one and the same
time there is all carnage
and blue-white prayer,
knifed flesh, cut bone, pure song.

The antithesis
of the dark red shout
is the air's silence,
still, blue-white,

ourselves shaped from stone –
in the morning,
tide-side an angel
watching us.

Under the wind
the beech hedge flickers.
By the tower
the wind blows dark grass.

In the morning
a whispered ebb
drowned by new glare
and a sharp song.

But past the tower
is rising ground,
democratic
light. No shadows.

Storm-Preaching on Pulpit Rock

Isle of Portland, Dorset

Beaks' snarl hallows beat of the cold front north-east.
Gulls on the Pulpit Rock evangelize spume,
invoke elements the coastguard sees civilised first
in barometer-fall, weather-change measure's worm.
Other priests come. Razorbills glare out
across water's whipping passionate church,
beseechment as demand summons Force Ten with a shout
cut jagged from Portland's edge on the brute-sacred perch.
No gentle pastoral prayer this, no consoling word;
beyond sight something is answering, something closes in,
by their voices they arouse an unknown, unnamed god,
chanting in a drowning scream of communion.
Gulls match voice-for-voice accelerating air,
the Word made storm, formed beyond Finisterre.

Nest

The night of pine trees
is self-fulfilling
circling a summit
on which an unspecied bird broods.

The lanes below weave
closer until the hill

is so present it is no longer
visible. The silence of the nest

remains guessed
but unwitnessed.

The needles
of old firs
shelter the young
in their dark.

Down from the hidden slopes

a stream
carries shell,
albumen traces.

One day what these
blind chicks will be.

Blue Poles
Jackson Pollock 1952

Make straight roads now.
The running colour is out of control.
Web, weave, weft –
once they were jazz, holy gothic, summer –
is it the black or the white light rushing up now?

The dark dripping into the day,
the light imploding down, down
and the colour in me waiting to pour out –
burst out – *Automobile Interior, 1956*,
red drying to black in a blinding white light.

Meantime what's missing here? The jazz of it.
I look down, you look across. What d'you think?
For sure the colours are out of control.
Make straight roads now. Find me a rhythm.
Eight straight roads to take us out of here.

Churchyard

August day.
English evening

yew trees.

A maze of table tombs'
eroding stone.

Yew trees.

Old stone
carvings fading to fog,

words gone far from their dead thought,
defeated by lichen.

Show me some sign. What point
is a grave without a message?

Here's just
A faint angel, man-made.

L'Ile Saint-Louis

After Alain Fournier

There is last light over the river.
Behind the old door, there are voices
carried on the wind, shared sounds,
the heard smile of a close promise,
but no one is there.

I can always recall how to reach this place.
I find it without thinking,
across water from a church, a bar's red canopy,
a glimpsed window beyond the footbridge,
a straight narrow street, a guitar.

I can of course never confront its prose.
I can never see it as fact, the account of it.
It is when said and done just memory:
not a place at all, just as Time
and time's young are nowhere.

Fournier's time before the Somme,
a light across the river, the tidal river
beyond the prose of it, the momentary spirit
caught by chance, the smile heard,
although no one is there.

But just sometimes the shadows shift
and there is a path down to a quay,
a footbridge, the whispering
of an empty room, a close promise,
behind a door, voices from nowhere.

SELECTED POEMS
(1981–1999)

From: *Figure in a Landscape* (1981)

Stone
i.m. A.L.S.

Your stone, small,
thrust like a piece of sky
sown from chinchilla clouds.

How the waters fled
over the skin of the stone,
glinting, smooth.

Heaven is like that.
Touch the stone,
feel it grow warm.

Half here, hatching,
half its bird flying,
spheres' egg links, splits.

Moss

The path has turned green overnight,
trees' colour drained, blood of leaves
soaking up from dead roots.

Smooth sense of place. Moss –
green soft word, the spread
of mould forming the sound.

Tread it, see it flex, a skin
regaining colour. It defies
us humbly but wholly.

Triangle

Something classic,
full of iced symmetry

stark on a pure white page
pyramid-confident.

Carve it sharp,
diamond-bright sides,
clean, clear, all angles
and thin lines.

No extras – a pointed tower
owning the space that surrounds it.

A cold cleansing,
a frost.

Tea at Monk's House

For Angelica Garnett

The garden patterns against the window,
colour from opaline leaves pressing through panes.

The glimmer of the underwater room is verdant,
a sea-orchard, cool, gathering fluid shadows.

Cups, fluted white shells, chink,
and the silver tea pot reflects as it tilts,

catches a diamond in the lush green light,
rich light where the slow dust swims.

The Return

"Tick" the clock whispers,
and the baby breathes
the feather-air through stillness....

On my shoulder a touch –
fragile snow – and I turn,
meeting invisible eyes.

The crib shimmers in warm light,
the room's normality murmurs,
merges with day's ebb.

And a girl, visiting the past,
looks back, brushing
through the whispering clock....

The air's soft down
Caresses the sleeping child. She stirs,
not wakes, but smiles in her dream.

Figure in a Landscape

Poplars absorb sky:
the blue blows through them,
they are awash with cool, coloured air,
they affect the spirit like church spires.

Yet I live in times
of earthquakes and wars:
there is always a reason for not
sleeping. Why concern myself with trees?

Peering into a
river, a calm stream,
my face fluctuates back up to me
just like a picture developing.

And it is itself
a glass and a book –
a harsh, sharp pen has scratched the mirror,
but it still echoes the blue poplars.

From: *Carvings* (1982)

La Grande Jatte, 1891

Together, they walked through the canvas…
it was Seurat's summer,
something inside the light danced,
pastels rippled across heat
from tuile and parasol
like lagoon coral.

Never did she dream she would cease to see
girls under dark trees, flowing ferns,
the park's bright light sifting,
the floss of the air's coloured snow,
the distant water's gild and spark
and before them as they walked, two shadows.

Tonight, the way she watches
these burnt paper birds
blown from chill shadows against the sky
empties her face, speaks clearly
that there is some new tomb I cannot see
in her sad heart's unmown grass.

Sisyphus

The caste of a beaten species upon him –
the Sisyphus syndrome, no contest.
And yet we all hold onto
some remembrances, a past.

So what can I say that's not a platitude?
I'm a stranger here myself,
both of us shadowed,
both sharing now and then a window.

True, hope reflects more than it shows,
in us, about us, beyond us.
But a sweet clear thing,
so many worlds at once.

So beyond platitudes I can say this:
looking at ourselves, there's a shared
glimpse of light through this clear glass.
Sisyphus, our shoulders are on the same stone.

Wood Sculptor

For John Fuller

Carving Time to reincarnate the tree –
travelling over circles to root's childhood, laterally.
Always the wood's past singing
I, musician, scribe and counterpart
to a song of severed rings
move into her heart
being born again in mutual striving.
And with this rebirth –
this bringing new life to old growth –
I find in the end myself to be
at once the fruit and harvester of every tree.

Persephone

After a wood carving by John Fuller

So proud, this harvester of golden fruit,
herself gathered up from Pluto's dark.
She holds the arrogance of warm fertility
in her eyes, in triumph's tilt of the neck.

Out of the underworld striding, amber queen
rising, the head opulent, unrepentant
slave, harlot and mother.
Persephone. Believe in the eyes' promise.

Year by year she returns like this,
the fresh light gleaming on the long back,
the body a reed fit for the wind's will,
out of man's dark dream a season of a woman.

Up Hades' stair no simple girl,
but given Demeter's gold
Goddess-strong and growing sun-vibrant,
coming full face to light, matching it.

A smile carving itself in new growth
and the emergent aureate skin matches day's bronzing.
Dark Dis buried a rich potent seed in that flesh,
and the girl's proud step bears up an invincible child.

Zoë
One Day Old

Close to strange unknowns,
distancing from them
you float fragile
in warm pools,
a little boat
pushed irrevocably out.

You passively rule us
from behind guru lids
where now and then
flashes sky like a memory –
signals from far beaches –
little Zoë, little Life.

Little life, waters' edge
blossom animate,
while distancing from unknown shores
you retain something of them for now.
New boat cast on deceptive shallows,
you bring us new life in your very name.

Seeing a Ghost

The light at the grey landing window,
a sheen on the stairs
made me look through you as you spoke.

You are a lived-in person,
always I am aware of the other side,
more felt than seen, but watching me too.

Apparently open, you open your heart,
and for a moment, I almost know you,
before the light shrouds down again.

And so we continue this charade,
each pulling away from the other's ghost,
living internally for preference.

Emotion does not enter into it,
things are clean and tidy between us,
the rooms we inhabit mutually unhaunted.

For our purpose it is satisfactory –
and if sometimes you too are troubled by a light
you almost see, you do not let it show.

From: *A Walk In Winter* (1989)

A Walk in Winter

It is a path yet to be followed, this broken road –
a cartway seen but not taken all these years,
even unthought of – unworthy of walking
on all but the worst days, when all else fails.

And now the ice digs deep, mud's hard edge
cuts at a stumble to bruise us blue,
but today it is a path to be followed
that the summer you saw, your last season, forsook.

The decaying fact of your absence freezes, stiffens –
holly blooms blood warnings in dishevelled hedges,
but flow and rot are suspended, held by the clamp of cold.
Nothing moves until a puddle cracks and water spills.

And over the hard calm curve of the winter down,
across the field, the lane's clear expectancy, there falls
last light from a sky of unshed snow,
fragile as frost's crisp feather on the rutted track.

Face

This is the landscape across which
we build dry walls, severing fields.
Rock strives up – this white bone – stitched

under hills' broken curve; age yields,
down where the line collapses, dies,
grows indistinct; watch how dusk builds

conscience heavy over it – skies
for a land shaped by being, all
these stones, these shadows, silent cries...

White-bones landscape – down hills, dry walls.

Morgan's Hill

For Desmond Hawkins

After the rain
a long view – and larks.
A climb through three gates,
but worth it for the best of Wiltshire.
We, surprised even now by this green antiquity
touching instinct, breathe in and smile.

And the sun points out meadows,
clouds paint themselves
and high Morgan's Hill sings a great wide song
to us until

we turn to the circle of trees,
and the hollow hauls us into itself.
A stump, scattered stones,
a fire's corpse and a stagnant pool;
a rook floats, sodden, swollen.
Here we are no longer part of things –
or part of something other.

We leave symptoms of ourselves everywhere.
Out there the winds dilute us.
Here, face to face with these echoes,
we fall silent.

Saddened, with nothing
but the rushing of beech about us,
we stumble out,
finding a sky we do not recognize
full of something darker than the rain.

Bird in a Church

There were white walls, there was invocation,
and out of the sun, fire came flying,
a second's sharp miraculous blaze
there on a candlestick, a flickering
to kindle the altar's purple torch.
At the turn of a full eye, vision
before the cerebrum's damp prose,
this flash through the stone dusk;
how the prayers burned,
how the dark flame fluttered!

Beach Building

On the winter shore they are remaking what years have undone.
While the grey light surges over horizon's hill,
they push a wedge into the sea – stone, wall – a groyne
through sand and shingle, a fence against sat water's will.

The litter of August, an inhabited promenade, are unimaginable today;
the blank cliff rings back as a pile drives down.
Undressed and empty, the tired resort gives way
to cold rain; behind the front, just another bleached-out town.

With giant stabs from sinking machines, men fight the incoming tide.
Long ago this place invented sand's presence as its reason for being,
and the longshore striving must at all costs be stayed
against the drift's advocacy, the waves' oblique instinct of freeing.

Here through the soft shale they have been vainly making
sheep-pens for distant fictions – carved in January, bulwarks
to hold summer fantasies – but the walls keep breaking.
Down on the winter shore, spring tides stalk our strongest works.

October 12*th*

All year it has been there, though hidden well,
looking like all the other numbers, just
waiting to be ticked with barely a glance,
a date to pass through, as we thought we must.

And yet now, see what it has done to us?
Just see what, all the time, it held in store:
a day to trip us, through remaining years.
How could we not have noticed it before?

The Leaves Are Down

The leaves are down from all but the cherry now.
The lawn grows autumn toadstools, fog falls, a frost,
the dark house gapes, the clocks go back, but
the cherry holds its leaves, refusing to believe in winter
even now.

Now

When friends ask, I go through it all again –
an autopsy on love, knowing now where to begin
where once I was wordless through obsequies
and the sharp recollection of lost intimacies.

Now the body, bound up with memory,
seems to hold its reality quite well, and I'm ready
for questions, can make a show of whether
I was right, and how and why, piecing it together.

So I go on digging my own sweet grave,
an Egyptian throwing in loved artefacts I've saved.
I rouge the dead cheeks, falsify the end;
once I was alive and wordless, now I can pretend.

From: *This True Making* (1992)

Snow

You and I there,
two very proper nouns,
saw the snow drift deep

below us,
the sliding hill
under a sun
managing
only moonlight.

We down the dry slope
waiting for reality
to envelope us.

Still the amazing light
hung, and we could not stop
our two brains believing,
our hearts ringing
with bright adjectives
until we came to the place
where there should
have been
snow.

Punctuation

We should notice
that a cat sleeping sometimes
is an apostrophe,
sometimes a full-stop,

that a dead vole
broken in a kestrel's claw
becomes a limp comma,
making a pause

in the bird's flight,
that there is in winter
daylight some sort of word
and in the night

punctuation
without thought, a silence
between stars, that it seems
the swim of a foetus

and corpse's attention are both
question and exclamation
framed in parenthesis.
Such metaphors

are our realities,
the encountering of
discovered synergies.
We should therefore

see ourselves just as marks
that might help some sense
of a sentence.
And strive to make shapes.

For Jeremy Hooker

Always this dancing: –
light through glass, chalk's ancient life,
Itchen growing towards tide
like the being in wood emerging –
always, always this dancing.

The still fragile act
of a poem begins here,
the spirit of place passed on
from a father's painter's eye intact,
and the past living as fact

to teach, informing
each day – a benediction
on all these things, like carving
that brings forth intact through a breaking
in the end this true making,

                    this dancing.

Fox

The fox that comes to my garden
seems oddly no longer alien.
I barely look up now,
though still aware
of a shadow.

The self I am offered
Fox chooses to adopt.
It is Spring, and among
erupting leaves the slim brush
slides, almost domesticating
the relaxing enemy
while sharpening
the very air around.

Under May's widening light
Fox pretends
a passionate sweetness
while scrawling a strange being
across the lawn,
becoming a part of it all.

Eye to eye,
we glory in this relationship.
Fixed by species
yet we are some sort of lovers now,
fear into lust
rippling over new grass,
a shining dusk on the move,
oscillation between fir trees.

Almost pet, always animal,
Fox captures a focus
like a red, red bud.
We are familiar yet awe-struck,
dying for a kill,
loving and losing one another
in twilight,

A Haunted House

A recalled essence – where the hosts
of long lost days glimmer – breeds mists,
perpetuates dusk, while silence
takes on a shape, looking askance

at us, hard, cold, its lonely eyes
 hidden. If there are any ways
for light, should it wish, to enter,
it barely does. Always winter

has a hold. Listen! Yes, something
spoke then – or perhaps softly sang
somewhere deep in the house – a voice
left behind, echoing like ice.

Caught in the act of their dying,
with the very walls decaying
into tears, rooms whisper last words
through twilight, while beyond their boards

outside the nervous air dances,
living things breathe. The place tenses
round us. We no longer belong.
This exorcism – the distant ring

of a step on dark stone, the strain
of an ear listening, sad thin
wisps of a past that glide and flow
over the dust – teaches no new

lessons but just reminds us how
to come to terms with it all, now
we are ghosts. This is how to die,
seeing light fail, sharing a sigh.

Poole Quay

Always for work, this old chipped wharf.
Poole wears water like a scarf
wrapped tightly round its throat,
hugging coal and crane, the summer boat,
ferry and all the habitually transient
against the quay's skin. Each vessel implements
the desire of history to be recalled: –
this stone wall has long excelled
at meeting the tide's volition,
countering it, turning it to tradition.

They would have understood, the old Poole men,
they would have smiled to watch us when
we look down the deeps of water at our feet,
knowing as we do that we meet
by implication every country's shore
that touches it, see in the port a whore
trading their harsh integrity
for the cold demanding bargain of the sea.

Always on the edge of tidescape,
clasped by Arne, Branksey and the steeps
of Purbeck against the shout of storm,
turning a back on farms for a life informed
by Ocean's huge uncertainties,
by distances' higher possibilities.

Two stars suddenly shine, green, red,
and now the water is inhabited.
We encounter another world, exchanging one
with Dorset islands for the harbour of St. John's.
Then, looking back, the ancient quay
becomes a haunted place; next, the fray
of breaker, storm and current: – will
enough to take us to their task. Ill
betide the man who looks behind him now…
Poole astern – towards Newfoundland the prow.

Statues in Bronze
For Elisabeth Frink

This king dies best with mist around him,
his dogs and horses strain to be away
and rolling again in the luscious dew.

On the hilltop they make the view
aware of their life... listen...
someone running...at the crest of a stride.

For these, landscape is no more just countryside
than sea is only water to a shore –
brute against grace, rock on the Down's curve.

The lawn is peopled, its preserve
being a place of essences,
the essence of being and place

with its own reality, face to face,
clubbing the slight with a mass
assertive as rough giants in chalk.

From: *Radio and Other Poems* (1999)

Shipping Forecast
Donegal

They have shared still late October,
but salt stones and a broken tree,
the peeled paint on the lifeboat house
chime with places where the glass falls,
prime sources encountering night's bald predictions.

Everywhere winter edges in,
and now the time is ten to six...

lightness and weight, air's potentials
pressed into words, implication;
here – on all coasts – listening grows passionately tense.

Fair Isle, Faeroes, South East Iceland,
North Utsire, South Utsire,
Fisher, German Bight, Tyne, Dogger...
This pattern of names on the sea –
weather's unlistening geography – paves water.
Beyond the music, the singing
of sounds – this minimal chanting,
this ritual pared to the bone
becomes the cold poetry of information.

The litany edges closer –
Lundy, Fastnet and Irish Sea...
Routine enough, all just routine.
Always his eyes guessing beyond
the headland, she perhaps sleeping, no words spoken.

He stretches forward to grasp it,
claims his radio place – *and now*
the weather reports from coastal stations
and then: *Malin Head* – such routine
that she barely glances up, but hears *now falling.*

Blue Candles

There had just been nothing but ice and iron
in the wind those first and last days.
Sick January – every breath fainter,
everything demanding your pain.

And then that night it was as if suddenly
blue candles were everywhere in the fevered room
and the frost on a translucent jug dripped
down starlight in a cool blue song.

Moon through Bristol Blue flowed into indigo,
the world sub aqua – aquamarine spilling
over us out of its brimming vessels
and in the heart of it a silver shine.

Blue light to salve the unquenched throat,
shadows to let cracked lips whisper.
And the candles burned their flowers,
turned their spirits to companionship,

out of their fuse murmuring a pool,
a new whole bright in deepest dusk,
velvet's touch against the eye's glaze
and the bead down the rich glass searching.

Outside the brute storm cutting,
its anger alive, jagged fact;
here the gradual trance of the soul's firework,
the liquid of these pastel diamonds,

these Gentians pouring their colour
while holding the argent sparkle
in an underwater darkness glowing,
growing until the pale morning came.

Above Newton Farm

Llansantffraed, Easter, 1995

Shadows and sun flicker across the valley,
silently questioning all false certitudes,
though I – full of new pictures – see beauty first.

I sit by a brook, grass is growing again
and in the next field on this renewed hillside
lambs leap; helplessly I think in metaphors.

It is so easy to imagine a man
singing in such a place, easy to believe
the loving witness of this weather, that words

could not grow from a stark doubt and duality,
from a cold loss and a bitter encounter,
not here where today I see only the sweet

dynamic of Spring light. Now in the next field
sheep are shouting, a cloud pauses while something
sends their panic spiralling to a vortex.

Quickly out of it and down the changing slope,
a ewe, dead giving birth, her lamb still-born, is
tractored away. The rest return to grazing,

sun resumes, the brook laughs. So – some answers?
Life's sure fact and the certainty of a tomb –
green under its tree – both cracked from side to side.

K595

Sometimes there breaks in on us a new dance,
darkness touched alight, something going straight
to the bone of our being. For instance,
circumventing thought, total and complete,
Piano Concerto Twenty Seven
unselves our worldliness, undoes our sleep,
a song brought back from the edge of Heaven,
a simple shape of notes that makes us weep.

Muire na nGael
Kildare – St. Brigid's Well

St. Brigid was born c.457, within the lifetime of St. Patrick.
She is revered as "Muire na nGael" – "The Mother of
Ireland".

From water to water, through stone stations,
fact, parable, all's one, no matter,

sacred thunder over the round tower
or horses on The Curragh, common ground.

Water, fire, a faint pagan mumble
through the fresh green cross;

here's no strangeness though sure enough –
Eternity's a silver note heard purely

in its own sweet time, go round listening,
but there's no hurry, God knows, don't rush,

Kildare can take its turn; Brigid's
safe meantime, a good strong woman,

so let's be practical too: look at the time,
there's time still, enjoy the crack,

you don't hurry saints, wait the day,
wait for the Guinness to settle to a drink.

Corpus Christi, Oxford

We two are walking, very late, in Merton Street.
We are talking, laughing, just ahead of the rest.
It is cool and I sense you feel it; placing
my jacket around you, I make a metaphor
for what I've never ever said. Surprising,
that moment now I think of it, not me at all,
the sudden tenderness of something almost lost;
and "You don't do things like that", I hear you thinking,
but it reminds us that I love you, so perhaps
there is hope – a man just now almost worth his child.

Charles Darwin at Down House, 1880

I ask you, what can I safely turn to now
that won't lead me on to unspeakable truths
squirming and screaming in some future darkness,
shuddering nightmares that the next century
will claim were my fault? Tell me, in my time left
under the village's trees, round the sand walk,
what's yet to find that won't wake me in the dark
with the congealing of its implication?
I pay for killing God with dying children;
what's to turn to safely these days – perhaps worms?

The Green Man is Drunk
From 'A History of The Green Man'

The lost art of it,
this drinking

begun without reason
or self-justification
is
made sacred by
the far truths, God

without an end – too much to bear

to be world without end.

How to live with that promise,
and the blackmail of nails in hands and feet –
make poems out of that Mister Green –
It drives you to drink.

And so I drink.

Building a Church, 1094
Christchurch, 1994

Christchurch Priory was built by Bishop Flambard, justiciar under
William II, who ministered to his king's excesses by oppressive
extortion of the people. The Priory has many legends, including the
story that its stones were moved during building from a nearby hill to
the present site between two rivers. Also that a mysterious workman
helped place a beam in position when no others could achieve it.

I realise that by now this has become an obsession –
the presence under the present on this
inhabited ground we reclaim with craft and sweat.
It is a walking side-by-side, ghost by ghost,
always a giant shadow, always a distant figure
lit by coloured air, obscured
by translucent dust in evening light,
so nearly seen.

We are always a pace behind
as we shape all this, ready
for monks to sing themselves
into its fabric. That is to come
when we have finished with it all;
as we carve the new, the stone we shaped
before grows old, grows mellow.

Outside the summer beats, the sunlight falls
on tourists pressing against ancient walls;
chip-grease and sun-oil stain miraculous stones
and paths are smeared with milk from ice-cream cones.

It has not been all prayer for us…
Flambard's smashings, there are many
would curse our new church,
the motive for all this.

But there is something about this light –
the motes in the sun
through half-finished glass,
the shadow of rainbows...

The toil of the place being born
obscures so much, the potential for silver sound,
the coolness when the dirt settles; so much to do,
but now look! The prayer of arches meting comes true,

is
answered.

*

The other Sunday trade is at the door,
it's summer, coach tour after coach tour:
fluorescent tee-shirts, sweating sandalled feet
stamping hard to make lost Sabbath hours complete.

We make the machine, it is for others
to make it work, to realise
the God in it, fuel
the engine of divinity we build
into its stones.

(If only they shall last down here
between water, so near to flood.
Sense put it on the hill,
deities can be perverse.

Deities and chancellors...)

I know by now this is a truth,
that before the shadow faded
we were present here, and by making this,
we have engaged the capacity
to be so forever.

Forget Flambard's funding tricks,
        what matters is what will be here,
        build something for God...
Keep composing the stone.

Make something for God.

They pick their trinkets from the Priory shop,
see the beam then wander round and drop,
drained by all this age into the nearest pub...
each to his own belief, particular club...

               *

Forget Rufus, Henry, black Flambard,
        think of the stones moving...
    think of the stone moving,
think how the beam fits now.

Here with the fabric of the present,
we build a new past, history's shaping,
something none but the dead can understand,

        the truth being
        only human
            after all.

A slow prevailing tide of time and changes,
a subtle song beyond the cross estranges
us from all that jars, which we mistake for vices –

like children on the gravestones eating ices...

Matins end, the faithful blink on out
into the sun; though ancient doors may shut
while worship lasts, we all are tourists really,
wait until collection's past, then austerely

stumble through the porch – as martens, residents
by squatters right sing frantic descants –
hand God back to the Philistine and go down
to pious lunch in the florid tempting town...

> the truth being
> only human

> > after all.

If it were only stone it would be as nothing.
For they will be fragile, these stones
that seem so much a part of eternity,
so preordained to be here,
they shall need love as we have loved them.

> We are the men who made this...hear us.
> It is this that links us –
> we are one across time –
> for what did we build
> if not for love?

Seek to walk within this house with a perfect heart,
but if you fail and are frail, fear not –
> the stones will understand.

> It is to do with burning an existence
> into life...so we live on in the coloured air.
> Like the light
> > the stones live on,
> > > we live on.
> > > > Listen. Can you not hear?
> > > > A long old song
> > > > > always beginning.

From
Rain Variations

I heard the boys in the street
kicking a ball in the rain,
heavy, hard rain. The ball hissed
at the dull thud of a foot
and I could see clearly
the bead-plume of water-drops
arcing as it spun silver
under the street's floodlights.
The rain beat against the glass.
The boys went on kicking ball
as the wet grew into dark.

Still Life

Evening light
through a gold wine,

arc of the horizon's still sea
and a civilised quiet – safe, clean –

inexplicable confederates
in the blue evening air,
summer's cool twilight veranda
shaped by the sunset

shadow over shadow,
the day's end's calm poignancy
and the tidal flow
come to a neap.

And here
were two with things shared who
watched idyllic distances fade
(and intentions with the wine's blooming),

and if they saw strange shapes in the glass –
worms hatching in the centre of living –
neither spoke of it:
they would not be party
to unborn dark angels –
they would not tonight

(though the interminable voice
beneath –
the black turn
of the larvæ –
nevertheless sang).

Three Yangtze Prints

After all, the year took back what I had thought were gifts.
(Lovers move out bit by bit). And I am left with this
empty winter room and the cold knocking of the wind.

Today's a test for poetry. The curve of the eye
towards the stars faltering half way catches itself
in damp broken apartments, the tired town's pale grey gloss.

This is when the right pictures on bedroom walls matter;
I've glanced at the prints you brought back from that
long-remembered
Yangtze trip too often as décor – now I take down

The Summer Palace for a closer look: a high bright
pagoda on a hill and glowing stone, a green slope,
a warmer blue – Time's persuasive old consolations.

And then there is this – *The Altar of Heaven* – circle
within perfect circle – six of them, aligned gates, soft
tints of pinks and mauves to ease this almost monochrome.

As always your true instinct offers me the answers.
I see *The Seventeen Arched Bridge* in its gentle light,
clear water, white reflections, an ice-span inverted.

Let the image grow from the innocent colour
as dark and bright abstractions empathise –
these blues, greens, just as they come,

let them influence this grey,

these pinks, mauves

white